THAT WHICH IS PERFECT

Pentecostal Gifts and the New Testament

THAT WHICH IS PERFECT
Pentecostal Gifts and the New Testament

by

John F Parkinson

RITCHIE

John Ritchie Publishing

40 Beansburn, Kilmarnock, Scotland

ISBN-13: 978 1 914273 42 1

Copyright © 2023 by John Ritchie Ltd.
40 Beansburn, Kilmarnock, Scotland

www.ritchiechristianmedia.co.uk

Typeset by John Ritchie Ltd., Kilmarnock
Printed by Bell & Bain Ltd., Glasgow

Contents

PREFACE

When the Lord Jesus ascended to heaven, He led captivity captive and gave gifts to men. We learn from the New Testament that the gifts were given by the Holy Spirit to the church on the day of Pentecost. Some of the gifts were for signs to the Jews, some were to reveal new truth, some were for evangelism, while others were for the building up of the church. There are differences among Christians as to which of these gifts are still current today. It is the standpoint of this book that the revelatory, miraculous, and sign gifts have ceased. We shall see that these gifts fell into disuse when "that which is perfect" had come. We contend "that which is perfect" refers primarily to the completed New Testament with its developed doctrine of Christ and His church.

By contrast, there are many Christians who believe that all the gifts of the Holy Spirit, without exception, are still current today. Those who take this position are normally known as Pentecostalists because of their belief that the church has the same gifts today as were given to it on the Day of Pentecost. The current Pentecostal and Charismatic phenomenon, with over 644 million adherents worldwide, is the fastest-growing religious movement in the world today[1]. It is therefore very important that we consider what the Bible teaches about the gifts of the Holy Spirit, as our understanding of the subject will impact on our gospel witness, our worship, and on our service. We trust that this presentation has been written in a spirit of respect, truth, and love. The book

---

[1] https:en.wikipedia.org/wiki/pentecostalism

is short and hopefully accessible to any interested Christian, irrespective of age, who is seeking to understand the "apostles' doctrine" more accurately on the gifts of the Spirit. May God grant us good understanding of His word.

I would like to thank all the friends who read the early drafts and who gave helpful feedback, especially Leslie Craig, Elton Fairfield, Brian Graham, Clark Logan (Botswana), Thomas McKillen, John Robert McLean (who has shared the thoughts of the late Davey Smith of Shetland), Noel McMeekin, Paul McMullan, John Mitchell, Craig Munro, and John Short (Hong Kong, China). Thank you also to Alison Banks and her colleagues at John Ritchie Ltd. Finally, a special thanks to my wife Andrea for her tireless support and invaluable help.

John F Parkinson
N. Ireland
2023

CHAPTER 1

THE PROMISE OF THE FATHER

- Tracing events from John's baptism to the Day of Pentecost

This study aims to examine the Scriptures concerning the momentous events that took place on the Day of Pentecost, as recorded for us in the second chapter of Acts. What was the promise of the Father and how are we to understand baptism with the Holy Spirit? What were the gifts of the Holy Spirit in the early church and, very importantly, what are the gifts of the Holy Spirit to the church today?

In this chapter, we shall look at the Scriptural usage and meaning of the much-misunderstood term of baptism with the Spirit. Many Christian friends understand this to mean that the Holy Spirit falls on a Christian as an extra blessing that comes later than conversion and that this baptism of the Spirit is evidenced by a new ability to speak in tongues. How should we respond to a new convert who says, "I have trusted Christ as my Saviour and am now waiting and praying for the baptism of the Holy Spirit"? We shall respectfully seek to show that this is a serious misunderstanding of the Scriptures. Comparing Scripture with Scripture, we shall endeavour to draw out the true meaning of what happened on the Day of Pentecost, and of what happens in our own day to sinners at the moment they trust Christ as Saviour.

When John the Baptist began his ministry to the nation of Israel, he urged the people to repent and prepare for the coming

Kingdom of God. Crowds from Jerusalem, Judea, and the region of Jordan flocked to hear him and were baptised in the River Jordan confessing their sins, among whom were common people, tax collectors, and soldiers. The Pharisees and Sadducees came to hear him but did not believe him (see Mt 21.25). Paul would later describe John's ministry in these words: "John verily baptized with the baptism of repentance, saying unto the people, that they should believe on him which should come after him, that is, on Christ Jesus" (Acts 19.4). What interests us in this opening chapter is what John had to say about a yet future baptism which would not be with water but would be with the Holy Spirit.

MATTHEW'S ACCOUNT
John the Baptist was the prophet of whom Isaiah wrote, "The voice of him that crieth in the wilderness, Prepare ye the way of the Lord, make straight in the desert a highway for our God" (Is 40.3). The long-promised Messiah was about to appear to the nation, and John was calling on the people to repent as the Kingdom of Heaven was at hand. Many people were baptised by John in the River Jordan, confessing their sins. While John was baptising with water, he made a prophecy that would eventually eclipse his own ministry, "I indeed baptize you with water unto repentance: but he that cometh after me is mightier than I, whose shoes I am not worthy to bear: **he shall baptize you with the Holy Ghost, and with fire**" (Mt 3.11).

There can be no doubt that John the Baptist was referring to Jesus of Nazareth when he spoke of the One who would follow him. The questions that now arise are how and when would the Lord Jesus baptise them with the Holy Spirit and with fire? At that time, it was still a future event.

The Lord Jesus also made His way from Galilee to Jordan to be baptised by John. Although He had no sin of His own, the Lord identified Himself with the repentant remnant of Israel and would in fact become their sin-bearer. This was a key moment that marked the beginning of the Lord's public ministry. Matthew records:

> "Then cometh Jesus from Galilee to Jordan unto John, to be baptized of him. But John forbad him, saying, I have need to be baptized of thee, and comest thou to me? And Jesus answering said unto him, Suffer it to be so now: for thus it becometh us to fulfil all righteousness. Then he suffered him. And Jesus, when he was baptized, went up straightway out of the water: and, lo, the heavens were opened unto him, and he saw the Spirit of God descending like a dove, and lighting upon him: And lo a voice from heaven, saying, This is my beloved Son, in whom I am well pleased" (Mt 3.13-17).

MARK'S ACCOUNT

Mark records John's words: "And John was clothed with camel's hair, and with a girdle of a skin about his loins; and he did eat locusts and wild honey; and preached, saying, There cometh one mightier than I after me, the latchet of whose shoes I am not worthy to stoop down and unloose. I indeed have baptized you with water: **but he shall baptize you with the Holy Ghost**" (Mk 1.6-8).

Mark also records the baptism of the Lord Jesus. Once again, the baptism with the Holy Spirit is referred to prophetically, i.e. as a future event.

JOHN'S ACCOUNT

Before considering Luke's extended treatment of the subject, we shall refer at this point to John's record. The Apostle John records for us John the Baptist's identification of Jesus as the Lamb of God. He recalls John's words: "And I knew him not: but he that sent me to baptize with water, the same said unto me, Upon whom thou shalt see the Spirit descending, and remaining on him, **the same is he which baptizeth with the Holy Ghost.** And I saw, and bare record that this is the Son of God" (Jn 1.33-34).

All four Gospel writers bear witness to John's words at the beginning of the Lord's public ministry, how that, at some unspecified time in the future, the Lord would baptise with the Holy Spirit. John, in his gospel, gives us further help in the understanding of the coming ministry of the Spirit. For example, at the Feast of Tabernacles, the Lord Jesus gives His great invitation to all in the temple, while John adds a piece of illuminating commentary:

> "In the last day, that great day of the feast, Jesus stood and cried, saying, If any man thirst, let him come unto me, and drink. He that believeth on me, as the scripture hath said, out of his belly shall flow rivers of living water. (But this spake he of the Spirit, which they that believe on him should receive: **for the Holy Ghost was not yet given; because that Jesus was not yet glorified**.)" (Jn 7.37-39).

This informs us that the Holy Ghost would not be given until the Lord Jesus would be glorified, i.e., after His ascension to heaven[1]. When we come to the upper room ministry on the night before the crucifixion, the Lord confides in His eleven apostles that He will be leaving them. They will not be alone, however, as He will pray the Father who will send another Comforter who will be with them and be in them: "And I will pray the Father, and he shall give you another Comforter, that he may abide with you for ever; even the Spirit of truth; whom the world cannot receive, because it seeth him not, neither knoweth him: but ye know him; for he dwelleth with you, and shall be in you" (Jn 14.16-17). The Lord Jesus repeats this promise that, when He has gone, the Father will send the Comforter, who is the Holy Spirit (Jn 14.26; 15.26; 16.7-16).

---

[1]What happened to those people who had heard and believed this promise of the indwelling Spirit, but had died before the crucifixion and resurrection of Christ? When did they receive this promise of the indwelling Holy Spirit? A most interesting explanation has recently come to my attention. The people referred to in Mt 27.52-53 were quite possibly those saints who were raised after the resurrection of Christ and who went into the Holy City appearing to many. Perhaps they too were baptised by the Spirit into the body of Christ on the day of Pentecost. I mention this without being dogmatic but offer it as a possible explanation of two otherwise puzzling verses.

Later that evening, at Gethsemane, the betrayal of the Lord Jesus initiated the terrible events which led to His death, burial, and resurrection. For forty days the Lord appeared at various times and places to His disciples. It is given to Luke to record His last appearance before ascending to Heaven.

LUKE'S ACCOUNT IN HIS GOSPEL
Having established the historical setting of John the Baptist's ministry in the time of Tiberius Caesar, Pilate, Herod, and the High Priests, Luke goes on to record the words of the Baptist: "I indeed baptize you with water; but one mightier than I cometh, the latchet of whose shoes I am not worthy to unloose: **he shall baptize you with the Holy Ghost and with fire**" (Lk 3.16).

The importance of this event is becoming very evident. Matthew, Mark, Luke, and John are united in drawing our attention to this future baptism of the Holy Spirit. Luke also records an event that took place about three years after the ministry of John. The resurrected Lord, speaking to the eleven apostles before leading them out to Bethany, says: "And, behold, I send **the promise of my Father** upon you: but tarry ye in the city of Jerusalem, until ye be endued with power from on high" (Lk 24.49).

LUKE'S ACCOUNT IN ACTS 1
Luke begins his second treatise to Theophilus (the book of Acts) by recording the Lord's last words to His apostles before His ascent to heaven. Notice that the baptism with the Holy Spirit, which was first spoken of three years earlier by John the Baptist, is now merely a matter of days away: "And (Jesus), being assembled together with them, commanded them that they should not depart from Jerusalem, but **wait for the promise of the Father**, which, saith he, ye have heard of me. For John truly baptized with water, but **ye shall be baptized with the Holy Ghost not many days hence**" (Acts 1.4-5).

The great event was to take place very soon. Firstly, the Lord Jesus would send the Holy Spirit from heaven to earth to permanently indwell His people - that is the promise of the Father. Secondly, His people would be baptised by the Holy Spirit into one unified body - that is the fulfilment of John the Baptist's prophecy. However, although all believers were both indwelt and baptised by the Holy Spirit, we judge that the accompanying signs would begin exclusively with the apostles only. The apostles knew that the event would take place "not many days hence". We now know it was ten days later. Meanwhile, Judas had been replaced by Matthias, and the twelve apostles were together in one place on the morning of the Day of Pentecost. A new dispensation of the Spirit was about to begin.

Before moving to events on the Day of Pentecost, the reader may be wondering why we have traced the 3-year timeline from the prophecy of John the Baptist to the Day of Pentecost. It is because we want to see clearly from the scriptures that the baptism of the Spirit is not an after-conversion experience repeated in the lives of some believers down through the ages, but is a unique and one-off historical event that happened on the Day of Pentecost. The baptism with the Holy Spirit was to do with the birth of the church and cannot be repeated.

CHAPTER 2

A SOUND FROM HEAVEN
- Discerning Events on the Day of Pentecost

The first four verses of Acts 2 are so important that we quote them in full:

> "And when the day of Pentecost was fully come, they were all with one accord in one place. And suddenly there came a sound from heaven as of a rushing mighty wind, and it filled all the house where they were sitting. And there appeared unto them cloven tongues like as of fire, and it sat upon each of them. And they were all filled with the Holy Ghost, and began to speak with other tongues, as the Spirit gave them utterance" (Acts 2.1-4).

This was the moment when the Holy Spirit descended from heaven to earth to permanently indwell every believer and baptise them into the body of Christ. This was the beginning of the church, His body. This new entity was something glorious and unprecedented. For the first time on earth, there were redeemed people who were not only individually indwelt by the Holy Spirit but were also united in one body, having been baptised by the Spirit into the body of Christ.

Paul would later write to the Corinthian believers and give the doctrinal meaning of what had happened: "For as the body is one, and hath many members, and all the members of that one body, being many, are one body: so also is Christ. For by one Spirit are we all baptized into one body, whether we be Jews or Gentiles, whether we be bond or free; and have been all made to drink into one Spirit. For the body is not one member, but many" (1 Cor 12.12-14). In other words, the Spirit is in us and we are in the Spirit.

It was during the 10 day interval, between the ascension of the Lord Jesus and the Feast of Pentecost, that Peter stood up among the 120 disciples (Acts 1.15) and spoke of the necessity of a replacement for Judas Iscariot who had not only betrayed the Lord but had also committed suicide. The replacement had to be a disciple who had followed in the company of the Lord and His disciples from the baptism of John to the resurrection and ascension of Christ. After prayer and casting of lots, Matthias was numbered with the eleven apostles, and so is included in the 'all' of Acts 2.1.

When the Day of Pentecost had fully arrived, we read that "they were all with one accord in one place" (Acts 2.1), meaning all twelve apostles. It is often assumed that the 120 disciples, mentioned in the previous chapter, were there, but the Scriptures do not say that. The narrative would seem to emphasise the unique role of the twelve. Although all the believers were baptised by the Holy Spirit into the body of Christ, almost certainly the tongues of fire and the speaking in foreign languages applied to the twelve Galilean apostles only.

The descent of the Spirit from heaven to earth was accompanied by a sudden sound from heaven as of a mighty, rushing wind, a sound which filled the house. There were also cloven tongues as of fire that sat on each of the twelve apostles. The next event was the sign which captured the attention of the inhabitants and visitors in Jerusalem. The apostles, now filled with the Holy Spirit, spoke in foreign languages as the Spirit gave them utterance.

The news of these startling events soon travelled around the city and multitudes of people made their way to the place to investigate. The crowds who came were confounded to hear their own languages and dialects being spoken by the apostles when proclaiming the wonderful works of God. Luke, the narrator, describes the scene:

"And they were all amazed and marvelled, saying one to another, Behold, are not all these which speak Galilaeans? And how hear we every man in our own tongue, wherein we were born? Parthians, and Medes, and Elamites, and the dwellers in Mesopotamia, and in Judaea, and Cappadocia, in Pontus, and Asia, Phrygia, and Pamphylia, in Egypt, and in the parts of Libya about Cyrene, and strangers of Rome, Jews and proselytes, Cretes and Arabians, we do hear them speak in our tongues the wonderful works of God" (Acts 2.7-11).

We cannot imagine the bewilderment experienced by the Jews on hearing the wonderful works of God spoken of, not in Hebrew, but in a wide variety of Gentile lanuages. The people were wondering what to make of such things. There was no natural explanation for this ability to speak in real foreign languages that they had never heard before. Standing up with the eleven apostles, Peter raised his voice and gave the explanation in his Pentecostal address. The phenomenon of tongues, he said, was what Joel had prophesied would happen in the last days when God would pour out His Spirit on all flesh. Although not all the signs that Joel predicted had yet happened, what they were witnessing was a foretaste of what would come in the last days, when there would be convulsive changes in the sun and the moon before the Day of the Lord. Peter then solemnly charged the people with the crucifixion of Christ: "Ye men of Israel, hear these words; Jesus of Nazareth, a man approved of God among you by miracles and wonders and signs, which God did by him in the midst of you, as ye yourselves also know: Him, being delivered by the determinate counsel and foreknowledge of God, ye have taken, and by wicked hands have crucified and slain: Whom God hath raised up, having loosed the pains of death: because it was not possible that he should be holden of it" (Acts 2.22-24). Continuing his gospel message, Peter explains the present postion of Christ and the new dispenstion of the Spirit, "This Jesus hath God raised up, whereof we all are witnesses. Therefore being by the right hand of God exalted, and having received of the Father the promise of the Holy Ghost, he hath shed forth this, which ye now see and hear" (2.32-33). He went on to speak of the resurrection of Christ and assured the people that God had made that same Jesus, whom they had crucified, both Lord and Christ.

The people who came to listen were convicted in their hearts that the tongues were a miraculous sign from God and asked Peter and the apostles what they ought to do. Peter urged them: "Repent, and be baptized every one of you in the name of Jesus Christ for the remission of sins, and ye shall receive the gift of the Holy Ghost" (Acts 2.38).

Notice that the offer of grace was to every one of them. That is wonderful. Through faith in Christ, they would receive the forgiveness of sins, and on believing would receive the gift of the indwelling Holy Spirit. Happily, there were about 3000 people that day who gladly received the word and were baptised, and such were added to the church. Further, we do not doubt that every believer in the Lord Jesus, wherever they were, including the 120 disciples in chapter one, and the 500 disciples in 1 Corinthians 15.6, also received the Holy Spirit on that day and were baptised by the Spirit into the body of Christ. In other words, those who had already put their faith in Christ before Pentecost received the Holy Spirit on the day of Pentecost, and those who trusted Christ on the Day of Pentecost also received the Holy Spirit on that same day.

Peter had been entrusted by the Lord Jesus with the keys to the kingdom of heaven, "Thou art Peter...and I will give unto thee the keys of the kingdom of heaven" (Mt 16.18-19). It was on the Day of Pentecost when Peter used the keys to preach the gospel to the Jews at Jerusalem and to usher in the day of grace or the age of the Spirit. Peter will use the keys a second time to confirm the Samaritans in gospel blessing, and again, a third time to open the door of gospel blessing to the Gentiles. This is no less than a momentous change from the ministration or dispensation of Law to the ministration or dispensation of the Spirit, i.e. a dispensing by God of the Spirit (2 Cor 3.6-8 KJV, cf RSV).

There was now something entirely new on earth, a company of people who were saved by the blood of Christ, indwelt by the Holy Spirit, and baptised by the Holy Spirit into the body of Christ. The gift of the Father was the descent of the Holy Spirit from heaven to earth. The baptism of the Spirit on the day of Pentecost was the beginning of the church, and as such could never be repeated.

It is important to note that the Son of God is presently seated at the Father's right hand in heaven, while the Holy Spirit is presently residing and ministering on the earth. The descent and baptism of the Holy Spirit cannot be repeated. Today, when a person puts their faith in Christ, they receive the Holy Spirit immediately on believing. There is no subsequent baptism, or 'second blessing' as some call it, of the Spirit. As already stated, on the Day of Pentecost, the Holy Spirit descended from heaven to dwell on the earth. To pray, in this present day, for the Holy Spirit to descend and fall on an individual or on a company of gathered people is to misunderstand what happened at Pentecost. The Holy Spirit does not descend from heaven again. He has already descended. When a sinner is saved today, he immediately receives the indwelling Spirit and is added to the church, His body, entering into the good of the work begun on the day of Pentecost.

We end this chapter by refuting a very common error. Many teach that the body of Christ was already complete on the day of Pentecost and consisted of all believers up to the rapture of the church. They argue that you cannot add to a body. Were present-day believers (including you and me) already members of the church, His body, on the day of Pentecost? Most certainly not. This is evident from the closing words of Acts 2.47 "And the Lord added to the church daily such as should be saved." In other words, when sinners believed the gospel, they were added to the church. It is the same for us today. When sinners believe the gospel, they are added to the church, His body. The adding to the church was not completed on the day of Pentecost because it is clearly recorded in verse 47 that it was happening on a daily basis. It is hugely problematic to hold that people in their sins were already baptised into the body of Christ back on the day of Pentecost. Paul reminded Gentile believers of their spiritual bankruptcy before they were saved: "That at that time ye were without Christ, being aliens from the commonwealth of Israel, and strangers from the covenants of promise, having no hope, and without God in the world" (Eph 2.12). How could these Gentiles, in their unconverted days, be described as 'without Christ' and 'having no hope' if they were already baptised into the body of Christ and added to the church before they were born? The plain meaning of verse 47 is that people were added to the church the moment they were saved. Today, as the gospel is preached, those who trust Christ are immediately added to the church. This will continue on a daily basis until the church is raptured.

Finally, there is much profit in considering the Feasts of Jehovah[1] that are so closely linked to our subject. There were seven annual Feasts of Jehovah, the first one being the Feast of the Passover. Historically for Israel, the Passover spoke of redemption out of

---

[1] See Table 3 *The Feasts of Jehovah*

Egypt; prophetically, it spoke of the death of Christ and redemption through His blood. It was no chance coincidence that the Lord Jesus was crucified on the Feast of the Passover. He was the true Passover Lamb to whom the Feast bore witness (1 Cor 5.7).

The day after the weekly sabbath following the Passover would have been the Feast of Firstfruits. Historically for Israel, the Feast was to honour God and thank Him for the harvest to come; prophetically, it spoke of the resurrection of Christ from the dead. How remarkable it was that Christ, who was crucified on the Feast of the Passover, rose from the dead on the Feast of Firstfruits. He was 'Christ, the Firstfruits' of whom the Feast was speaking (1 Cor 15.23).

Seven weeks after the Feast of Firstfruits, on the day after the Sabbath, was the Feast of Pentecost. Fifty days would run their course from First Fruits to Pentecost. Historically for Israel, Pentecost was an opportunity to give God thanks for the wheat harvest; prophetically, it spoke of the coming of the Holy Spirit and the formation of the church. The Lord Jesus appeared in resurrection for the first 40 days and then ascended to heaven from the Mount of Olives. Ten days later, when the day of Pentecost had fully come, the apostles were gathered together in one place to wait for the baptism of the Holy Spirit and the promise of the Father.

There were three Feasts out of the seven which were obligatory for every male in Israel to attend: Passover, Pentecost and Tabernacles. As a consequence, during Passover, Jerusalem would have been crowded with people, many of whom would have witnessed the crucifixion of Christ. Similarly, fifty days later, Jerusalem would again have been crowded with people who would have witnessed the many wonders and signs done by the apostles. Invisibly, every believer in the Lord Jesus was indwelt by the Holy Spirit and baptised into the body of Christ. God was working in grace to the great timetable of the Seven Feasts of Jehovah.

CHAPTER 3

THE GIFTS OF THE HOLY SPIRIT
- Teaching the Apostles' doctrine to the first-generation church

By the time the Day of Pentecost had run its course, there were over 3000 believers in the Lord Jesus Christ. Presumably many were inhabitants of Jerusalem, while many were visitors who had travelled from foreign places to attend the feast. The question which then arose was: what would they do next? How would they organise and how would they know what to teach?

The only Scriptures that the believers had on the Day of Pentecost were the Old Testament Scriptures. The new converts were already familiar with the Law of Moses, the Psalms and the Prophets, these being read in the synagogues every Sabbath day. The Old Testament, however, does not include a developed doctrine of Christ and His church. Given that the New Testament Scriptures had not yet been written, how would these early believers be instructed in Christian doctrine? The answer to that question is answered clearly and is worthy of careful consideration. In those early days, the responsibility and authority for doctrine and practice lay firstly with the apostles who had been empowered and appointed for this foundational ministry to the church, and secondly with prophets. Paul would later explain to the Corinthians, "And God hath set some in the church, **first apostles, secondarily prophets, thirdly teachers**, after that miracles, then gifts of healings, helps, governments, diversities of tongues" (1 Cor 12.28). Paul also explained to the Ephesian believers that the church was "...built upon **the foundation of the apostles and prophets**, Jesus Christ himself being the chief corner stone" (Eph 2.20). We shall look firstly at the foundational gift of the apostles.

'FIRSTLY APOSTLES'

We receive a helpful indication in Acts chapter 2 regarding the activities of those new believers from the Day of Pentecost onwards. We read:

> "Then they that gladly received his word (Peter's) were baptized: and the same day there were added unto them about three thousand souls. And they continued stedfastly in the **apostles' doctrine** and fellowship, and in breaking of bread, and in prayers" (Acts 2.41-42).

Notice (v.41) that there are two things that happen only once in the life of a believer and which are not repeated: saving faith and believer's baptism. There are also four ongoing activities (v.42) that will be repeated many times during the life of a believer in conjunction with the local church: the apostles' doctrine (Bible study and teaching), fellowship, breaking of bread, and prayers. These are two key verses that succinctly and simply set the pattern for all time regarding the composition and practice of a local church in accordance with the New Testament.

So how did the apostles receive their doctrine? Let us listen to the Lord Jesus preparing His apostles for the great task ahead. How could they possibly remember everything that the Lord had taught them during those three years? How could they carry on without the Lord being with them? In the upper room ministry (John chapters 13-17) the Lord advised the eleven that He must leave them, but that He would send a Comforter who would be with them and in them. Let us follow the teaching of the Lord Jesus concerning the promised ministry of the Holy Spirit.

THE HOLY SPIRIT'S TEACHING MINISTRY (John 14.26)

The apostles in the upper room must have feared for the future. How could they teach others about things they did not understand? The answer, of course, is that the Spirit would teach them all things, and bring to their memory the things which the Lord had said. "These things have I spoken unto you, being yet present with you. But the Comforter, which is the Holy Ghost, whom the Father will send in my name, he shall teach you all things, and bring all things to your remembrance, whatsoever I have said unto you" (Jn 14.25-26). This is vital to remember today concerning studying and teaching the Bible. Without the Holy Spirit, we cannot understand the scriptures. Speaking of the things of God, Paul states: "*Which things also we speak, not in the words which man's wisdom teacheth, but which the Holy Ghost teacheth; comparing spiritual things with spiritual*" (1 Cor 2.13).

THE HOLY SPIRIT'S TESTIMONY TO CHRIST (John 15.26)

For the second time in the upper room ministry, the Lord Jesus refers to the Holy Spirit as the "Spirit of truth" (Jn 15.26).[1] The Spirit of truth shall testify to Christ: "But when the Comforter is come, whom I will send unto you from the Father, even the Spirit of truth, which proceedeth from the Father, he shall testify of me." This testimony would undoubtedly include His Deity, holy humanity, virgin birth, sinless life, atoning death, bodily resurrection, ascension to God's right hand, and His second coming. The Spirit of God does not point to a religion or philosophy but always points to Christ. With the help of the Spirit of God, the apostles were to preach and teach Christ. We are to do the same.

---

[1] The other two references to the Spirit of truth are in 14.17 and 16.13.

THE HOLY SPIRIT'S MINISTRY TO THE WORLD (John 16.7-11)

The question arose in the hearts of the disciples as to why the Lord Jesus had to leave them at that time. The Lord explained that it was better for them if He left them (v.7). On the one hand, if the Lord did not leave them, the Spirit could not come to them. On the other hand, if the Lord did leave them, He would send the Holy Spirit to be with them. It would no longer be necessary for an anxious soul to come to Jerusalem to seek the Lord. The message of the gospel now goes out to all people everywhere, while the Spirit of God indwells every believer no matter in what part of the world they might reside.

The Lord went on to explain what the Spirit's ministry would be to a sinful world. Firstly, He will convict the world of sin. Man's sinfulness must be understood before there can be any sense of need on the sinner's part. Otherwise, they will remain in their unbelief. Secondly, the Spirit will convict the world of God's righteousness. That is the foundational truth about God which, for Paul, is the starting point of the gospel message. God is righteous and men are sinful. Thirdly, the Spirit will convict the world of judgement. In other words, He shows men that they are *condemned* sinners. God is the moral Governor of His creation and He will judge sin. People know that their deeds condemn them, either by the Law or by their God-given conscience (see Rom 2.12-16). The gospel is the message for guilty sinners. No one can be saved apart from the Spirit's work, but this must not be seen as a limitation upon grace or on the scope of the gospel. Happily, the Spirit has come so that none need perish. The Spirit's present ministry is to convict the **world** of sin, righteousness, and judgment.

THE HOLY SPIRIT'S TEACHING ON THINGS TO COME (John 16.12-13)

The apostles could not possibly have understood and imbibed the whole body of truth on that night in the upper room (v.12). The

Lord Jesus told them that the Spirit of truth would guide them into all truth. The Spirit would not speak independently but would teach what He had heard from the Father. One of the important themes of the Spirit's teaching would be *"things to come"* (v.13). This included the prophetic book of Revelation. John, having been exiled to the Isle of Patmos, records: *"I was in the Spirit on the Lord's day"* (Rev 1:10). The Spirit showed John future events concerning the Messiah, Israel and the nations, while teaching about the millennial kingdom and the eternal state.

THE HOLY SPIRIT'S GLORIFICATION OF CHRIST (John 16.14-15)
The ultimate and highest ministry of the Spirit, if we may speak in such terms, is to glorify the Son. The Lord Jesus said: *"He shall glorify me: for he shall receive of mine, and shall shew it unto you"* (v.14). All things that the Father has belong to the Son, and the Spirit takes those things and shows them to us. When we meet to remember the Lord Jesus in the breaking of bread, the Holy Spirit leads us in worship and shares with us God's thoughts about His Son.

THE APOSTLES' AUTHORITY (John 20.21-23)
The above commands of the Lord Jesus were given on the night before the crucifixion. At the core of the teaching was the coming of the Holy Spirit to be with them and in them. He would teach them all things they needed to know. But there is also an anointing with the Spirit which took place on the evening of Resurrection Sunday when the Lord appeared in the locked room where ten of the apostles were present. How would the apostles be sure that they had the authority to speak on the behalf of Christ, and how would the people know that the apostles had such authority? The Lord Jesus said to the apostles present, "Peace be unto you: as my Father hath sent me, even so send I you" They will be going forth with the authority of Christ. The Lord then gave them apostolic power and authority which was unprecedented:

"And when he had said this, he breathed on them, and saith unto them, Receive ye the Holy Ghost: Whose soever sins ye remit, they are remitted unto them; and whose soever sins ye retain, they are retained". It is important to understand that this was not the baptism of the Spirit that would unite all believers on the Day of Pentecost. We suggest that this pre-anointing was the bestowing of apostolic authority, preparing the apostles for that great commission of being sent out by the Lord, just as the Father had sent Him out. Firstly, they would be empowered to make authoritative judgements based on the terms of the gospel, and secondly, to judge governmentally in church matters, e.g. in the case of Ananias and Sapphira (Acts 5.1-11). Without a doubt, Thomas, who was missing that evening, would also have received the same empowerment eight days later.

An interesting question now arises. How were the believers on the Day of Pentecost to know that the twelve apostles had been vested with special authority and power by the Holy Spirit of God? Why should anyone, believer or unbeliever, take their claims seriously? That question is easily answered. On the Day of Pentecost, when the Holy Spirit descended to earth with a sound from heaven as of a rushing wind, the apostles could hear the sound and could see the cloven tongues as of fire sitting on each of them. Regarding the people, they heard these same Galileans speaking in languages that were foreign to them, clearly a miraculous event. When Peter gave his Pentecostal address, he stood up with the eleven, identifying with them as the twelve chosen apostles of Christ. There could be no doubt to anyone, except for the mockers, that the twelve apostles were appointed, empowered, and authorised by God.

If further proof were needed of the authority of the twelve apostles, we read: "And fear came upon every soul: and many wonders and signs were done by the apostles" (Acts 2.43). Taught in the school of Christ and empowered by the Holy Spirit to preach and teach, the apostles laid the foundations of Christian doctrine in those early days following Pentecost. The foundational work of the church was carried out, first by apostles and secondly by prophets.

'SECONDLY PROPHETS'

What is a prophet? Following the sound principle that the Bible is its own interpreter, we shall look for answers from the scriptures. Peter wrote: "For the prophecy came not in old time by the will of man: but holy men of God spake as they were moved by the Holy Ghost" (2 Pet 1.21). An Old Testament prophecy was not the product of a man's imagination but a message that came directly from God to the prophet who would, in turn, convey it to the intended person or persons as moved by the Holy Spirit. The letter to the Hebrews begins with this opening truth: "God, who at sundry times and in divers manners spake in time past unto the fathers by the prophets, hath in these last days spoken unto us by his Son..." (Heb 1.1-2). God used prophets to speak to past generations but now has spoken in His Son. The Lord Jesus said: "For all the prophets and the law prophesied until John" (Mt 11.13; Lk 16.16). John the Baptist was the last and the greatest of the Old Testament prophets.

When the risen Son of God ascended to heaven, He led captivity captive and gave gifts to men. Among those gifts to the church, given by the Holy Spirit, were apostles, prophets, evangelists, pastors and teachers (see Eph 4.7-12). A New Testament prophet was a man of God who received messages directly from God and, as moved by the Spirit, shared them with the early Christians. The messages may have been doctrinal revelations or they may have been predictive prophecies. Bearing in mind that at that time there were no New Testament scriptures and that there were only twelve apostles, the role of the prophets would have been very important in disseminating new Christian doctrine.

The Old Testament prophets had a ministry concerning Israel and the coming Messiah. The New Testament prophets had a ministry to do with the Church and its risen Head. How would this new order of prophets serve the church? We read in Acts chapter 11 of prophets coming from Jerusalem to Antioch and prophesying of coming famine, an example of predictive prophecy. This resulted in relief being sent from Antioch to Jerusalem. In Acts chapter 13 we read that in the church that was in Antioch there were certain prophets and teachers. Importantly, these prophets received doctrinal revelations to pass on to the saints. For example, when Paul told the Ephesians that Gentiles would be fellow heirs in the same body, he made reference to both apostles and prophets: "How that by revelation he made known unto me the mystery; (as I wrote afore in few words whereby, when ye read, ye may understand my knowledge in the mystery of Christ) which in other ages was not made known unto the sons of men, **as it is now revealed unto his holy apostles and prophets by the Spirit**; that the Gentiles should be fellow heirs, and of the same body, and partakers of his promise in Christ by the gospel" (Eph 3.3-6).

The two foundational gifts to the church were the apostles and prophets. We mention at this point that the apostles would all necessarily die and that prophecies would cease. We shall return to this issue in due course. The next gift on the list is teachers.

'THIRDLY TEACHERS'
The importance of teaching could hardly be overrated. The church at Antioch, often regarded as the first Gentile assembly, had a number of prophets and teachers: "Now there were in the church that was at Antioch certain prophets and **teachers;** as Barnabas, and Simeon that was called Niger, and Lucius of Cyrene, and Manaen, which had been brought up with Herod the tetrarch, and Saul (Acts 13.1). Paul later told Timothy: "And the things that

thou hast heard of me among many witnesses, the same commit thou to faithful men, who shall be able to teach others also" (2 Tim 2.2). Every local church was to encourage those with the gift of teaching to teach others also. This is a gift that must be developed today by study. It's not possible to expound the scriptures if you are not studying the scriptures. It is important to note that the gift of teaching is current today, unlike prophecy which has ceased.

'MIRACLES, THEN GIFTS OF HEALING, HELPS,GOVERNMENTS, DIVERSITIES OF TONGUES'

We are confining ourselves, for the time being, to the day of Pentecost and the days immediately following Pentecost. During that time, the gifts of the Spirit could be divided into three main groups: **foundational gifts**, **grace gifts and sign gifts**. Foundational gifts are those given to the apostles and prophets to teach authoritatively the doctrine and practice of the early church. By grace gifts, we mean those which build up and strengthen the saints, while sign gifts are those which testify mainly to the Jewish nation.

Among the sign gifts were miracles, healings and tongues. We have already noted that in Jerusalem "many **signs and wonders** were done by the apostles" (Acts 2.43). Miracles and healings were numerous in those early days following Pentecost:

> "And by the hands of the apostles were many **signs and wonders** wrought among the people... insomuch that they brought forth the sick into the streets, and laid them on beds and couches, that at the least the shadow of Peter passing by might overshadow some of them. There came also a multitude out of the cities round about unto Jerusalem, bringing sick folks, and them which were vexed with unclean spirits: and they were healed every one." (Acts 5.12, 15-16).

The apostles had been speaking in foreign languages which could be understood by visitors to the city, and this was followed by miracles and healings. These signs were bearing witness to the truth that Jesus of Nazareth had risen from the dead. Jerusalem had never seen signs on this scale. The gift of tongues was another mighty sign to the Jews.

To enable us to understand the gifts of the Spirit it is vital for us to follow events through the Acts of the Apostles. It is helpful to remember the Lord's words to the apostles before He ascended to heaven: "But ye shall receive power, after that the Holy Ghost is come upon you: and ye shall be witnesses unto me both **in Jerusalem, and in all Judaea, and in Samaria, and unto the uttermost part of the earth**" (Acts 1.8). We have observed the events in Jerusalem, noting the descent of the Holy Spirit from heaven to earth and the baptism of believers by the Spirit into the body of Christ. We have also noted, very importantly, that the Holy Spirit gave gifts to men. Some of these gifts were for signs to the people of Jerusalem, and some were to confirm and build up the believers in their faith. We shall continue our study by following events from Jerusalem to Judea and Samaria.

'IN ALL JUDEA AND IN SAMARIA'

After the martyrdom of Stephen, there was a persecution of the Christians in Jerusalem so that all the church, except for the apostles, was scattered into Judea and Samaria. Those who were scattered went everywhere spreading the gospel. Philip (the evangelist, not the apostle) made his way to a Samaritan city and preached Christ to them. The Samaritans believed the gospel when they saw the miracles of healing and the casting out of demons. When the apostles in Jerusalem heard about Samaritans receiving the word of God, they sent Peter and John to investigate. Interestingly, the Holy Spirit had not yet fallen on these Samaritan believers, even though they had been baptised in the name of the Lord Jesus. There had evidently been a work of regeneration in their hearts but they had not yet been permanently indwelt by the Spirit. It was not until Peter and John had prayed and laid their hands on them, that they received the Holy Spirit. This was the second time that Peter used the keys of the Kingdom of Heaven, opening gospel blessing to the Samaritans. It is important to note that Philip had neither the power or authority to lay his hands on the Samaritan believers so that they would receive the Holy Spirit. Only the apostles were empowered to do so. This authority, which was used again by the apostle Paul in Ephesus (Acts 19.6), was exclusively the remit of apostles. This unique apostolic authority ended with the passing of the apostles. The idea that there are apostles alive today who can lay their hands on people to receive the Spirit has no Scriptural warrant. In this present day, the person who believes in Christ for salvation receives the Holy Spirit at that very same moment of faith.

There is yet another reason why it was necessary for the Samaritans to receive the Holy Spirit at the hands of the apostles from Jerusalem. Historically, the Samaritans had their own religion, temple and altar. The woman of Samaria had said to the Lord Jesus: "Our fathers worshipped in this mountain; and ye say, that in Jerusalem is the place where men ought to worship." The Lord responded: "Woman, believe me, the hour cometh, when ye shall neither in this mountain, nor yet at Jerusalem, worship the Father. Ye worship ye know not what: we know what we worship: for salvation is of the Jews. But the hour cometh, and now is, when the true worshippers shall worship the Father in spirit and in truth: for the Father seeketh such to worship him. God is a Spirit: and they that worship him must worship him in spirit and in truth" (Jn 4.20-24). The woman was betraying a Samaritan mindset, thinking that the Samaritan religion was as good as and equal to the Jewish religion. The Lord disillusioned her by affirming that Samaritan worship was sheer confusion, and that salvation was of the Jews.

This was a critical and glorious moment for Peter and John and the Samaritan believers. The Lord's words were being fulfilled – the hour had come when the true worshippers would worship the Father in spirit and in truth. But again, we ask why must it be that they would receive the Holy Spirit at the hands of the apostles from Jerusalem? We suggest that when the Samaritans submitted to Peter and John, they were acknowledging that Samaritanism had always been wrong and that indeed salvation was of the Jews. Significantly, by receiving the Holy Spirit at the hands of the apostles, they were accepting the apostles' doctrine. There could never be two churches on earth, one for Jews and one for Samaritans. The Samaritans could never claim that they had their own Samaritan church with its own apostles and its own doctrine. Initially, the Samaritan believers received the Holy Spirit at the hands of the apostles from Jerusalem. From that moment on, future Samaritan believers would receive the Holy Spirit immediately on believing. In fact, there would be no difference between Jews and Samaritans. The Jewish believers and Samaritan believers were now united, without distinction, in the one unified body of Christ.

It is important to pause here and make some observations about the laying on of hands. The apostles, and only the apostles, were able to impart the Holy Spirit by the laying on of their hands. These were special cases in the early apostolic church. Apostolic power was not passed on to the next generation. Defining the meaning of LAYING ON in his dictionary, W.E. Vine has written[2]: "A laying on of hands by **the apostles**, accompanied by the impartation of the Holy Spirit in outward demonstration, in the cases of those in Samaria who had believed, Acts 8.18; such supernatural manifestations were signs especially intended to give witness to Jews as to the facts of Christ and the faith; thus

---

[2]From entry for 'LAYING ON' in W.E. Vine, *Expository Dictionary of Bible Words*

they were temporary; there is no record of their continuance after the time and circumstances narrated in Acts 19, **nor was the gift delegated by the apostles to others**" (emphasis added).

The truth about the apostles' unique authority to impart spiritual gift by the laying on of their hands is also demonstrated in the case of Timothy. Paul was encouraging Timothy to stir up "the gift of God, which is in thee by the putting on of my hands" (2 Tim 1.6). Paul also exhorted Timothy not to neglect the gift that had been given to him by prophecy, and which was endorsed with the laying on of the hands of the eldership (1 Tim 4.14). Vine helpfully explains: "In 2 Tim 1.6 the apostle states that the impartation of the gift of God was through the laying on of his own hands. In 1 Tim 4.14 the preposition "with" indicates that his act was accompanied by that of the presbytery, or elders, by the way of ratification. The laying on of hands [of an apostle] was an outward sign of the bestowal of a spiritual gift. In the act of the presbytery it was a token of their identification with Timothy in his calling."[3] In short, it was the apostle who was the channel for the God-given gift, while the elders were merely recognisng Timothy's gift and calling.

Today there are no apostles or prophets. There is no one in the church today who can impart blessing or healing by the physical laying on of their hands. **In the case of assembly elders today, with the whole assembly, commending a believer to the Lord's work, the laying on of hands is no longer physical but is a figure of speech denoting spiritual recognition and united fellowship.**

Before leaving Samaria, we want to notice a beautiful work of grace that God had done in the heart of the apostle John. There was a time when he looked on Samaritans as utterly useless and only fit to be destroyed. His Jewish anti-Samaritan prejudice ran

---

[3] W.E. Vine, from comments on 1 Tim 4.14 in Collected Writings of W.E Vine, Vol. 3.

very deep. On one occasion John and his brother James proposed to the Lord that they destroy a whole Samaritan village with fire. The Lord Jesus responded: "Ye know not what manner of spirit ye are of. For the Son of man is not come to destroy men's lives, but to save them" (Lk 9.55-56). Now we see John back in a Samaritan village, this time praying for the people, not that they would be destroyed, but that they would receive the Holy Spirit. Surely the apostle John, when he saw the blessing among the Samaritans, would have remembered the Lord's beautiful words of grace and life. What a Saviour!

'UNTO THE UTTERMOST PART OF THE EARTH'

We have reached a point in the narrative where Jews and Samaritans receive the Holy Spirit immediately on believing. We now turn to the case of the Gentiles to ascertain what stage the first Gentile believers received the Holy Spirit. Peter had fallen into a trance and saw a great sheet lowered down from heaven with all manner of animals and birds, many of which would have been unclean to a Jew. A voice told him: "Rise, Peter; kill, and eat" (Acts 10:13). When Peter protested, the voice said: "What God hath cleansed, that call not thou common." This was repeated three times. The next day Peter and six brothers from Joppa made their way to Caesarea accompanying the men who had been sent by Cornelius, the Roman centurion. On entering the home of Cornelius, Peter realised the full meaning of the previous day's vision – that God was no respecter of persons and that He would save both Jews and Gentiles without favouritism. Peter then preached Christ to the gathered company of Gentiles, ending his address with the words: "To him give all the prophets witness, that through his name whosoever believeth in him shall receive remission of sins" (Acts 10.43). For the third and last time Peter was using the keys of the kingdom - this time to open the door of gospel blessing to the Gentiles.

While Peter was still speaking, the Holy Spirit fell on all those who were listening. It was a moment of astonishment for Peter and his Jewish brethren to realise that the gift of the Holy Spirit was also poured out on the Gentiles. This was not a second descent of the Holy Spirit from heaven to earth, but rather the Holy Spirit, who had already descended to earth on the day of Pentecost, was now poured out on the Gentiles. Was there a sign for Peter and his brethren that such a blessing had really happened? Indeed there was: "For they heard them speak with tongues, and magnify God" (Acts 10.46).

It is interesting to note that, unlike the Samaritan believers, the Gentile believers did not receive the Holy Spirit at the hands of the apostles. Peter observed that Cornelius and his Gentile friends had received the Holy Spirit just as the Jewish believers had at the beginning. Peter then commanded that the new Gentile believers, who had received the Holy Spirit, should be baptised in water in the name of the Lord. We can now see the future pattern for all believers being established – **the moment that sinners, whether Jews, Samaritans or Gentiles, believe in the Lord Jesus Christ, they immediately receive the indwelling Holy Spirit and are added to the church, the body of Christ, coming into the good of the baptism of the Spirit which took place on the day of Pentecost. This is followed by water baptism in the Lord's name. This scriptural pattern is normative for all today.**

When Peter returned from Caesarea to Jerusalem he gave an account to the apostles and brethren. Some were hard to convince that uncircumcised Gentiles could be saved and blessed on equal terms with Jews. Peter recalled how Cornelius had told them that an angel had instructed him to send to Joppa for Peter, "who shall tell thee words, whereby thou and all thy house shall be saved" (Acts 11.14). This news must have been music to the ears of Cornelius. Peter related what happened when he preached Christ: "And as I began to speak, the Holy Ghost fell on them, as on us at the beginning. Then remembered I the word of the Lord, how that he said, John indeed baptized with water; but ye shall be baptized with the Holy Ghost. Forasmuch then as God gave them the like gift as he did unto us, who believed on the Lord Jesus Christ; what was I, that I could withstand God?" (Acts 11:15-17). The Gentiles had believed on the Lord Jesus Christ, and the Holy Spirit had fallen on them. For the benefit of these believers in Jerusalem, Peter equated this event with what John the Baptist had predicted. The Lord Jesus Christ had baptised these Gentile believers with the Holy Spirit into the body of Christ. From that moment, Gentiles who put their faith in Christ would immediately receive the Holy Spirit on believing.

The reaction of the apostles and brethren in Jerusalem to Peter's report on events in Caesarea was that of silent wonder and praise: "When they heard these things, they held their peace, and glorified God, saying, Then hath God also to the Gentiles granted repentance unto life" (Acts 11:18). This is a critical moment in the early life of the church. Jewish believers have learnt that Gentiles are saved by faith in Christ and indwelt by the Holy Spirit in exactly the same way as themselves. They will soon learn a further truth about the body of Christ, a mystery hidden in other ages but now made known by the Spirit to the holy apostles and the prophets, that the Gentiles should be fellow-heirs, and of the same body, and partakers of His promise in Christ by the gospel (Eph 3.1-7). We shall return presently to Paul and his apostleship.

There was still one more group of disciples who had yet to receive the Holy Spirit. When Paul arrived in Ephesus on his third missionary journey, he discovered twelve Jewish disciples living in the city. On asking if they had received the Holy Spirit, Paul was informed by them that they had never even heard of the Holy Spirit. On learning that they were baptised unto John's baptism, Paul explained: "John verily baptized with the baptism of repentance, saying unto the people, that they should believe on him which should come after him, that is, on Christ Jesus" (Acts 19.4). On hearing Paul's words they were baptised in water in the name of the Lord Jesus. Paul then laid his hands on them and the Holy Spirit came on them. Was there a sign for Paul and his brethren that such a blessing had actually happened? Yes indeed! We read that they spoke with tongues and prophesied. Why was it necessary that Paul would lay his hands on them? As believing Jews, receiving the Holy Spirit at the hands of the apostle would have been a submission to the apostles' doctrine and authority. They had been baptised by the Holy Spirit into the body of Christ.

This meant that all four believer-groups described in Acts were now baptised into the body of Christ. The four groups were:

1) **Believing Jews**, who received the Holy Spirit on the day of Pentecost. These included the twelve apostles and all those in other places who had already believed in the Lord Jesus (Acts 2).
2) **Believing Samaritans**, who received the Holy Spirit at the hands of the apostles from Jerusalem (Acts 8).
3) **Believing Gentiles**, who were in Caesarea in the house of Cornelius and who received the Holy Spirit immediately on believing in the Lord Jesus (Acts 10 and 11).
4) **Believing disciples of John**, who received the Holy Spirit at the hands of the apostle Paul (Acts 19).

It has been helpfully pointed out that these were not four baptisms, but one baptism in four stages, until all four believer-groups had been included. On the return of Christ to heaven, the promise of the Father was to send the Holy Spirit down from heaven on the

Day of Pentecost to be with the believers, to be in them, and to baptise them into one unified body. The formation of the church, His body, constituted one unique event which cannot be repeated. The baptism with the Holy Spirit united all believers, without distinction, into the body of Christ, the church. Paul told the Ephesian believers that there is "One body, and one Spirit...One Lord, one faith, one baptism" (Eph 4.4-5). Everyone today, upon believing, is incorporated into His body and added to the church. Some employ the expression "baptised with the Spirit" to mean this incorporating into the body. We repeat that the baptism of the Spirit on the day of Pentecost cannot be repeated *insofar as the formation of the church is concerned.* Nor is it repeated in the experience of a Christian after conversion. The Holy Spirit does not come down from heaven to earth again, because He is already here.

Paul told the Ephesian believers: "In whom ye also trusted, after that ye heard the word of truth, the gospel of your salvation: **in whom also after that ye believed [or upon believing], ye were sealed with that holy Spirit of promise,** which is the earnest of our inheritance until the redemption of the purchased possession, unto the praise of his glory" (Eph 1.13-14). The logical order is 1) you heard, 2) you believed, and 3) you were sealed. 'After that ye believed' means 'immediately upon believing'. Logically the believing came before sealing, but practically they were instantaneous. Paul wrote to Roman believers and stated: "Now if any man have not the Spirit of Christ, he is none of his" (Rom 8.9).

It is now time to turn our attention to the apostle who was as one born out of due time – Paul, the apostle to the Gentiles.

PAUL, APOSTLE TO THE GENTILES

The twelve apostles and the people listed in 1 Corinthians chapter 15 saw the Lord Jesus in His resurrection appearances before and up to the event of His ascension to heaven. There was, however, one notable exception. The last person on the list, Paul the writer, did not see the Lord during those forty days. After stating "And last of all he was seen of me also", Paul describes himself as one born out of due time, being the only person to see the Lord Jesus after His ascension. The others had walked and talked and even eaten with the risen Lord who was not yet glorified. But when the Lord Jesus appeared on the Damascus Road to Saul of Tarsus, there was a light from heaven brighter than the noonday sun. It would seem that the Father had already glorified His Son. The light blinded Saul. In his testimony to King Agrippa, Paul told of the commission he received from the glorified Lord: "And I said, Who art thou, Lord? And he said, I am Jesus whom thou persecutest. But rise, and stand upon thy feet: for I have appeared unto thee for this purpose, to make thee a minister and a witness both of these things which thou hast seen, and of those things in the which I will appear unto thee; delivering thee from the people, and from the Gentiles, unto whom now I send thee, to open their eyes, and to turn them from darkness to light, and from the power of Satan unto God, that they may receive forgiveness of sins, and inheritance among them which are sanctified by faith that is in me" (Acts 26.15-18).

During the lifetime of the apostles, the New Testament was being written gradually, book by book and letter by letter. The letters (epistles) of the apostle Paul are particularly important in relation to the gifts of the Holy Spirit. We can clearly discern a shift in emphasis from the early letters to the later letters[4]. There are four lists of spiritual gifts in the New Testament, and it is important to observe the distinctions in emphasis. J.M. Davies has helpfully pointed out that the list of spiritual gifts given in 1 Corinthians is not only the longest of the four lists, but is also the earliest in time, and so includes the miraculous and sign gifts. The list in

---

[4]For a chronology of all the New Testament literature see Table 2.

Romans comes later and is reduced to seven in number. The list in Ephesians, which comes latest in order of time, is different in that the gifts are the men given to the church for its edification. Davies explains, "In this (Ephesians) passage, written some years later still, there are but five listed, two of which are said to be connected with the laying of the doctrinal foundation, leaving three gifts which are permanent, viz. the evangelist, the pastor and teacher."[5] An appreciation of these shifts in emphasis will give us the key to discern which gifts have ceased and which gifts continue to this day. Peter's shorter list is to do with service.

Concerning the gifts, the four lists which concern us most are found in the following letters:
- 1 Corinthians, written by Paul about A.D.57 from Ephesus
- Romans, written by Paul about A.D.58 from Corinth
- Ephesians, written by Paul about A.D.62-63 from Rome
- 1 Peter, written by Peter about A.D. 62-64 from Babylon

First List
1 Corinthians 12.7-11. Wisdom, knowledge, faith, healings, miracles, prophecy, discerning of spirits, tongues, and interpretation of tongues.
Also verse 28. Apostles, prophets, teachers, miracles, healing, helps, administrations, tongues.

Note the inclusion of prophecy and knowledge, as well as miracles and tongues. These were vital for the early church. Prophecy and knowledge were to reveal and explain doctrine, while tongues was a sign to unbelievers (1 Cor 14.22). These were temporary gifts until the New Testament would be completed, at which time the gifts of prophecy, tongues and knowledge would fade away and cease (1 Cor 13.8-10). We shall return to the subject of sign gifts shortly.

---

[5]From J.M. Davies, *The Christian's Statue of Liberty* in "Collected Writings of JM Davies" Vol 1 p.464.

Second List

Romans 12.6-8. Prophecy, ministry, teaching, exhortation, giving, ruling (leading), and showing mercy.

The list is now reduced to seven, without reference to the miraculous or sign gifts.

Third List

Ephesians 4.11. Apostles, prophets, evangelists, pastors and teachers.

The apostles and prophets were foundational gifts to the church (Eph 2.20 and 3.5). The ministry of the prophets and apostles was to lay the doctrinal foundations of the church, a work that was completed in their lifetime. We now have the whole Bible, consisting of the Old and New Testaments. The canon of scripture is complete, and there is no more revelation. That leaves three permanent gifts in the church today: evangelists, pastors, and teachers.

Fourth List

1 Peter 4.9-11. Hospitality, speaking, and ministering (serving).

These are gifts of service. Every believer has received a gift so that we can serve one another. It is most interesting that Peter, the chief apostle and spokesman on the Day of Pentecost, makes no reference whatever to the miraculous gift of healing or to the sign gift of tongues!

WHAT NEXT?

Inevitably, there came a day when the last of the apostles died. How would the next generation of God's people remember the apostles' doctrine? The answer is that the next generation of Christians, and every subsequent generation up to the present day, would have 'that which is perfect' - the inspired New Testament scriptures. Further, they would have the indwelling Holy Spirit to teach them. We shall now turn our attention to the issue of teaching the apostles' doctrine to our own generation.

CHAPTER 4

THE NEW TESTAMENT SCRIPTURES

- Teaching the Apostles' doctrine to succeeding generations

In our consideration of the gifts of the Holy Spirit during the lifetime of the apostles, we discovered from the scriptures that, broadly speaking, there are four categories of gifts:

1) **Foundational gifts**, e.g. apostles and prophets
2) **Sign gifts**, e.g. miracles, healing and tongues
3) **Grace gifts**, e.g. evangelists, pastors, and teachers
4) **Service gifts**, e.g. hospitality, speaking, and serving

We have proposed in this study that foundational and sign gifts have ceased, while grace gifts and service gifts are current today. On what do we base this distinction? Can we point to any scripture that would teach that some gifts would cease while other gifts would continue? This is a very important question to which we answer yes:

> "Charity never faileth: but whether there be **prophecies, they shall fail**; whether there be **tongues, they shall cease**; whether there be **knowledge, it shall vanish away**. For we know in part, and we prophesy in part. But when that which is perfect is come, then that which is in part shall be done away" (1 Cor 13.8-10).

In chapter 12 of the same letter, Paul has been teaching that there is a diversity of gifts but the same Holy Spirit. To certain people, the Spirit has given different gifts to benefit all the saints. But great as those gifts might be, they must be practised with love (*KJV*, charity), otherwise, a person will be nothing better than a noisy gong or a tinkling cymbal. Paul states that in contrast to some gifts, love will never pass away. What are the gifts that will pass away? In verse 8, Paul names three gifts which were to cease, viz. prophecies, tongues, and knowledge. Why should these gifts vanish, while others do not? As these verses are critical to our understanding of gifts, we shall take a closer look at their nature and purpose.

1) PROPHECIES SHALL FAIL

A prophet is someone who receives revelations directly from God to pass on to other people as instructed by the Holy Spirit. The genuine prophet was able to say "Thus saith the Lord". We noted earlier that the last of the Old Testament prophets was John the Baptist. When the Holy Spirit descended on the Day of Pentecost, He gave gifts to men, including the gift of prophecy. Apostles and New Testament prophets are the two groups whose work is referred to as foundational (see Eph. 2.20). The twelve apostles had been with Christ for three years and were official witnesses to His resurrection. They were uniquely empowered by the Holy Spirit to remember and teach all that Christ had taught them. On certain occasions, apostles (and only apostles) could lay their hands on converts so that they would receive the Holy Spirit. When the apostles died, their foundational work was finished. There was no apostolic succession.

There were also prophets gifted to teach and pass on messages from God in matters of doctrine and practice. This oral ministry of prophets was necessary until all the revelations were written down in inspired writings. When that would happen, prophesying would pass away. When would that happen? The answer is 'when that which is perfect is come.' What are we to understand by such words? We contend 'that which is perfect' is the inspired and inerrant New Testament, (see later, page 50) which contains the full revelation of Christ and His church. The Old and New Testaments together make up the whole Bible, comprising the full canon of scripture. The need for prophetic revelation no longer exists. Today, prophecies have passed away, and both Old Testament and New Testament prophets are redundant.

2) TONGUES SHALL CEASE

Speaking in tongues is a hotly debated topic today and there is much confusion about this gift. It is very important, therefore, to understand the scriptural usage of tongues. There were legitimate and helpful ways to speak in tongues, but there were also selfish and unhelpful ways. It was a gift that could easily be abused. Paul writes extensively about tongues and we do well to give heed.

On the Day of Pentecost, the Holy Spirit fell on all believers, but it was the twelve apostles only who were associated with the cloven tongues, as of fire, that sat on each of them. They were filled with the Holy Spirit and spoke in other languages which were understood by the many visitors to Jerusalem. It was not humanly possible for twelve Galileans to know so many foreign languages. They were not only foreign languages, but they were *Gentile* languages. The events on the day of Pentecost were, firstly, a witness or sign to the Jews that God had made Jesus, whom they had crucified, both Lord and Christ. Secondly, the events were also signs to confirm to the believers that the Holy Spirit had come. Later, at the conversion of Cornelius and the Gentiles, their speaking in tongues was taken by Peter as a clear sign that the gift of the Spirit was also poured out equally on the Gentiles (see Acts 10.45). Later still, in Ephesus, when Paul laid his hands on the disciples of John, the Holy Spirit came on them and they spoke with tongues and prophesied (see Acts 19.6).

Apart from the Acts of the Apostles, the only other book that deals with tongues is Paul's First Letter to the Corinthians. In his list of gifts, he mentions two which go together: "to another **divers kinds of tongues**; to another the **interpretation of tongues**" (1 Cor 12.10). Paul goes on to point out that there is a variety of gifts, but that no one person has all the gifts. He asks: "And God hath set some in the church, first apostles, secondarily prophets, thirdly teachers, after that miracles, then gifts of healings, helps, governments, diversities of tongues. Are all apostles? are all prophets? are all teachers? are all workers of miracles? Have all the gifts of healing? do all speak with tongues? do all interpret?" (1 Cor 12.28-30). Paul urges the readers to desire and value the best gifts. Listing the gifts in order of importance at that time, he starts with apostles and prophets as the most important, and ends with the least important - speaking with tongues and interpretation. He claims there is a more excellent way, and leads the readers into the beautiful commendation of faith, hope and charity in the much-loved chapter 13.

It is, of course, in chapter 13 where Paul tells us that tongues shall cease, the main reason being that tongues and interpretation of tongues are sign gifts. Today they are no longer necessary. Even though tongues are now obsolete, Paul has still quite a lot to say about their proper usage at that time which has very practical lessons for us today. He begins chapter 14 with an exhortation to follow love and to desire spiritual gifts with a definite preference for prophecy. Why should prophecy be better to follow than tongues?

Firstly, Paul advises that unknown tongues are not understood by men but by God, whereas prophesying is speaking to men for their edification, encouragement and comfort. Speaking in an unknown tongue edifies oneself, while he who prophesies edifies the church. So Paul wants our participation to be for the good of the church, and not just for oneself. While the gift of tongues was still operative there was evidently some edification to the speaker himself, but if there was no interpreter, the tongues were of no value to the church!

Secondly, he urges that we speak in words that are easily understood. Even though tongues and prophecy have passed away, we can benefit greatly by taking Paul's advice to the first generation church and applying it to assembly life in our own generation:

1) Those taking part in an assembly meeting should make sure that what they are saying is for the good of the whole assembly and not just for the satisfaction of the speaker. It is good to remember that the ultimate goal of all ministry is to produce Christ-likeness in the saints. The ministry should be for the good of others and not for oneself. What applied to the prophet in the first generation church applies to the teacher in the present-day church.

2) Those taking part in an assembly meeting should make sure that they use words that can be understood. Paul writes: "So likewise ye, except ye utter by the tongue words easy to be understood, how shall it be known what is spoken? for ye shall speak into the air" (1 Cor. 14:9). What an excellent rule for everyone who takes public part in assembly meetings! Use vocabulary that all can understand. Avoid academic or technical language. Paul writes: "Yet in the church I had rather speak five words with my understanding, that by my voice I might teach others also, than ten thousand words in an unknown tongue" (14.19). The contrast

between five words and ten thousand words is so striking that it renders any comparison almost meaningless! If this is important for the ministry of the word, how much more important is it for the preaching of the gospel?

If tongues have ceased, what was their purpose in the first place? Paul gives us a clear answer to that question: "In the law it is written, With men of other tongues and other lips will I speak unto this people; and yet for all that will they not hear me, saith the Lord. **Wherefore tongues are for a sign, not to them that believe, but to them that believe not**: but prophesying serveth not for them that believe not, but for them which believe. If therefore the whole church be come together into one place, and all speak with tongues, and there come in those that are unlearned, or unbelievers, will they not say that ye are mad?" (1 Cor 14.21-23). This could hardly be clearer. The original purpose of the gift of tongues, therefore, was to be a sign to unbelievers, whereas the purpose of prophecy was to instruct believers. On the original Day of Pentecost, the twelve Galilean apostles spoke of the works of God in numerous Gentile languages, a sign that would have astonished and shocked the Jews. Even so, the majority of Jews refused to hear what was an unmistakable sign from God.

Notice also that there was to be orderly and considerate conduct during a meeting of the church: "Let the prophets speak two or three, and let the other judge. If any thing be revealed to another that sitteth by, let the first hold his peace. For ye may all prophesy one by one, that all may learn, and all may be comforted. And the spirits of the prophets are subject to the prophets. For God is not the author of confusion, but of peace" (1Cor 14.29-33a). Now here is something that we should all ponder, that **the spirits of prophets are subject to the prophets!** That rules out being 'slain in the Spirit' and other trance-inducing activities. We cannot worship God in a trance. The worshipper was to sing and pray with his understanding. The prophet was always to be in control of his speech and behaviour. That is worth thinking about.

Many people take verse 39 of 1 Corinthians chapter 14 as the scriptural mandate to prophesy and speak in tongues in the present time: "**Wherefore, brethren, covet to prophesy, and forbid not to speak with tongues**". Why was Paul refusing to issue a prohibition on tongues? There was no need to prohibit tongues because they were about to cease. We suggest that he had no desire to divide the Corinthian assembly over something that was about to cease. He urged them to earnestly desire to prophesy, knowing that the prophet would soon be replaced by the teacher. In terms of edifying the church, prophecy was the best of the gifts whereas speaking in tongues was the least of gifts. So again we ask why didn't Paul simply forbid tongues? Again, the answer is in chapter 13. The Corinthian assembly was very volatile and carnal. There were already enough divisions within the assembly over other matters. There was nothing to be gained by adding another potential point of division over a minor gift that would soon pass away.

Further, there is also the possibility that there was still a purpose in tongues at Corinth, namely to convince the unbeleiving Jews in the area. Therefore, to have forbidden speaking in tongues prematurely might have caused some to miss salvation.

When would tongues cease? They would cease whenever that which is perfect had come, viz. the New Testament. If we are permitted to paraphrase Paul's words, we suggest he was saying something like this: "There is no need to forbid speaking in tongues because their purpose and value is coming to an end. They are of very limited value, but to forbid them at this stage could cause needless problems within the assembly. Besides, when that which is perfect comes, tongues shall cease as a gift of the Spirit. In the meantime, there is nothing to be gained by forbidding them". We suggest that verse 39 of 1 Corinthians chapter 14 must be read in light of verse 8 of chapter 13.

3) KNOWLEDGE SHALL VANISH AWAY

We understand this gift to be divinely-imparted knowledge or understanding of spiritual truth, particularly Christian truth. Normally, knowledge is acquired by studying and learning. Before the writings of the New Testament, however, there would have been no opportunity to acquire knowledge of Christian doctrine by studying. The temporary gift of knowledge compensated for this deficit until the New Testament became available, by which time, or shortly thereafter, the gift of knowledge would have vanished.

"THAT WHICH IS PERFECT"

Paul explains that these temporary gifts provide nothing more than a partial understanding of Christian truth. Are we given any indication when these particular gifts would cease? These particular gifts would be done away with when "that which is perfect is come" (1 Cor 13.10). What does Paul mean by "that which is perfect"? It almost certainly refers to the perfect and inspired writings of Matthew, Mark, Luke, John, Paul, Peter, James and Jude. **In other words, the New Testament writings comprise the completed and perfect revelation of Christian doctrine, and so supersede the pentecostal gifts of prophecy, tongues and knowledge**. The New Testament is the apostles' doctrine ratified in written form.

To be fair, there are some good and respected commentators who, although agreeing that certain gifts have ceased, do not consider "that which is perfect" to be the New Testament. They see it exclusively as the eternal and heavenly state. Notwithstanding, it is the view of this writer (and of many other commentators), that the thought flow running through 1 Corinthians chapters 12, 13 and 14, overwhelmingly demands "that which is perfect" to be primarily the completed New Testament. Taken together with the Old Testament, the whole Bible is the complete canon of scripture, the inerrant and inspired word of God. Paul explains that when he was a child, he spoke as a child, he understood as a child, he thought as a child, but when he became a man he put away childish things. So it is with Christian revelation. Those gifts, such as tongues, prophecy and knowledge, belonged to the childhood stage of Christian knowledge. Putting away the childish things, we can now embrace the mature and perfect teaching of the completed Bible. There are no more revelations to the church.

Discussions on the meaning of 'that which is perfect' are often polarised by taking an either/or approach (i.e., either completed scriptures or eternal state). W.E. Vine very helpfully suggests a both/and approach rather than an either/or approach. Commenting on Verses 9 and 10, Vine writes:

> **"For we know in part, and we prophesy in part: but when that which is perfect is come, that which is in part shall be done away**. – there is stress upon "in part" in each clause. The statement in verse 10 holds good in whatever respect it may be applied; it is applicable to the temporary nature and partial scope of the supernatural gifts (ver. 8). With the completion of Apostolic testimony and the completion of the Scriptures of truth ("the faith once for all delivered to the saints", Jude 3 R.V.) "that which is perfect" had come, and the temporary gifts had been done away. For the Scriptures provided by the Spirit of God were "perfect". Nothing was to be added to them, nothing taken from them. This interpretation is in keeping with the preceding context.

It is also true that "that which is perfect" is to be brought in at the Parousia of Christ when the church is completed and caught up to be with Him. That which is partial will then be done away. Then the perfect will be substituted for the partial[1]."

Given that we now have the full quota of scriptures in the Bible, and that there is no new revelation of spiritual truth, what are the gifts of the Spirit that are operative today? The last list of gifts by Paul is in his letter to the Ephesians:

"And he gave some, apostles; and some, prophets; and some, **evangelists**; and some, **pastors** and **teachers**; for the perfecting of the saints, for the work of the ministry, for the edifying of the body of Christ" (Eph 4.11-12).

Paul has already described the apostles and prophets as foundational (Eph 2.20). This leaves the three main grace gifts to the church today as evangelists, pastors and teachers. These gifts are for the perfecting of the saints, for the work of the ministry, and for the edifying of the body of Christ.

EVANGELISTS

An evangelist is gifted by the Holy Spirit to preach the gospel of Christ to the unsaved and to win souls for the Saviour. There were those who were clearly designated as evangelists such as Philip, who was identified as "Philip the evangelist, which was one of the seven"(Acts 21.8). For an example of Philip's gospel preaching to a town see Acts 8.5, where we read that Philip went down to the city of Samaria and preached Christ unto them. For an example

---

[1]Vine, W.E., on 1 Cor. 13.9-10 in *The Collected Writings of W.E.Vine Volume 2* (Gospel Tract Publications, Glasgow, 1985) pp. 149-150.

of Philip's gospel preaching to an individual see Acts 8.26-40, where we read that Philip, drawing from Isaiah 53, witnessed to the Ethiopian eunuch by preaching unto him Jesus.

Timothy, who evidently had the gift of an evangelist, was instructed by Paul, "But watch thou in all things, endure afflictions, do the work of an evangelist, make full proof of thy ministry"(2 Tim 4.5). This provides an excellent focus for our main task in an ungodly world – preach the gospel! It is not our task to Christianise society by political activism. Our task is to preach Christ. A major activity of every local assembly ought to be the furtherance of the gospel. When a local assembly arranges gospel meetings, they should make sure that the invited speaker clearly has the gift of an evangelist.

PASTORS

A pastor is a shepherd, one who has been gifted by the Holy Spirit to lead, tend, protect and sometimes correct the flock. Whereas an evangelist interfaces with the world of sinners, a pastor works among saints like a shepherd among sheep. Elders are to feed the flock of God which is among them, willingly leading them with a ready mind, being examples to them (see 1 Pet 5.1-4). This pastoral gift will normally be evident in several brothers in an assembly, but all the elders should certainly be gifted pastors. An elder who has no pastoral gift would be an anomaly. Each assembly should have a plurality of elders, each with a shepherd's heart. The modern idea of a single titled pastor or minister over a whole congregation is not found in scripture.

TEACHERS

A very important gift to the church today is that of the teacher. The Holy Spirit has gifted some to study and expound the scriptures. The church was built on the foundation laid by the apostles and prophets, Jesus Christ Himself being the chief cornerstone. For the first generation church, the apostles' doctrine was taught orally by the apostles themselves as well as by prophets and those with the gift of knowledge. When that first generation died out, who would carry on teaching the apostles' doctrine? Jude tells us that we should "earnestly contend for the faith which was once delivered unto the saints" (Jude 3). It is no longer a case of memory (as it was for the apostles) or fresh revelations of truth (as in the case of the prophets), but we now have the inspired New Testament writings which, together with the Old Testament, tell us all we need to know. It is not prophets who are needed today, but teachers who will study the Bible and expound it to others. Whereas a prophet would have received a direct revelation from God to proclaim to others, the teacher must study the scriptures to pass on the doctrine to others with the Spirit's help. Paul told Timothy: "Study to shew thyself approved unto God, a workman that needeth not to be ashamed, rightly dividing the word of truth" (2 Tim 2.15). You cannot be a Bible teacher if you do not study the Bible.

The three main grace gifts in operation today are:
1) the evangelist, who preaches Christ in the gospel;
2) the pastor, who serves Christ by caring for the sheep;
3) the teacher, who instructs about Christ from the Scriptures.

All of these gifts must be practised with faith, hope and love, the greatest of these being love. There are also service gifts that are mentioned by Peter and are still current today: "Use hospitality one to another without grudging. As every man hath received the gift, even so minister the same one to another, as good stewards of the manifold grace of God. If any man speak, let him speak as the oracles of God; if any man minister, let him do it as of the ability which God giveth: that God in all things may be glorified through Jesus Christ, to whom be praise and dominion for ever and ever. Amen" (1Pet 4.9-11). Every believer receives one or more gifts from God and they should endeavour to discover them and practise them in a spirit of stewardship and joy. We must not neglect the gift that is in us. We can conveniently divide Peter's list into three:

1) Hospitality – This is the kindness that is shown, without resentment, to others who are in need of friendship and refreshments. Women are particularly gifted in this service.

2) Speaking – This is the privilege of every man in fellowship to speak publicly in assembly life, passing on thoughts from the word of God. This should be done reverently, remembering that he is handling the Word of God. It is also the privilege of every believer to speak in a personal capacity, either witnessing or helping someone in their personal need. There is constant need for public ministry and there is the occasional need for personal counselling.

3) Service – Anyone who does any service for the Lord and His people should do so with all the strength that God provides. This will bring glory to God through Jesus Christ. Peter ends his section on the gifts with an uplifting doxology: "to whom be praise and dominion forever and ever. Amen" (1 Pet 4.11).

At this stage we shall summarise our conclusions by asking two questions. Firstly, what gifts of the Spirit are in current usage today? Secondly, how can we know the apostles' doctrine today? The answer to the first question is that the main grace gifts today are those of the evangelist, the pastor. and the teacher. The service gifts of hospitality, speaking and serving are also current today. The answer to the second question is that we have the New Testament, which together with the Old Testament, gives us the full revelation of the apostles' doctrine.

It is worth remembering that in Old Testament times, the Spirit of God was active both in creation (Gen 1.2; Ps 104.30) and in the sovereign control of world history (Isaiah 40.7, 13). God, by the Holy Spirit, spoke to Israel by the prophets (Zech 7.12; 1 Pet 1.11). Regarding the Spirit's ministry to individuals, we read that the Spirit *came upon* men, e.g. Othniel (Judg 3.9) and Samson (Judg 14.6). Equally, the Holy Spirit could *depart from* men, e.g. Saul (1 Sam 16.14). David prayed that God would not take the Holy Spirit from him (Ps 51.11). The Holy Spirit could leave individual servants if they were not faithful to the commands of God.

In Old Testament times the first temple in Jerusalem, built by King Solomon, was to be God's dwelling place, but was destoyed by the Babylonians because of Israel's unfaithfulness. The second temple, built by Zerubbabul and later enhanced by Herod, was destroyed by the Romans in A.D.70.

By contrast, in New Testament times the Holy Spirit came down to be with His people and in them forever, just as the Lord Jesus had explained in the upper room ministry. This promise was fulfilled on the Day of Pentecost when believers in Christ were indwelt individually and baptised by the Holy Spirit into one unified body, the church.

Today, in the figurative language borrowed from the temple, the Holy Spirit indwells:

1. The church corporate (Eph 2.20-22)

"And are built upon the foundation of the apostles and prophets, Jesus Christ himself being the chief corner stone; In whom all the building fitly framed together groweth unto an holy temple in the Lord: In whom ye also are builded together for an habitation of God through the Spirit."

2. The local church (1 Cor 3.16)

"Know ye not that ye are the temple of God, and that the Spirit of God dwelleth in you?"

3. The individual believer's body (1 Cor 6.19)

"What? know ye not that your body is the temple of the Holy Ghost which is in you, which ye have of God, and ye are not your own?"

This promise is of tremendous comfort to the believers of this church age. The Holy Spirit is with us, in us, and will never leave us. The world neither receives Him, sees Him nor knows Him. On the other hand, the Christian knows Him because "he dwelleth with you, and shall be in you" (Jn 14.17). Not only are believers indwelt by the Spirit, but they are also born of the Spirit (Jn 3.5); sealed by the Spirit (Eph 1.13); led and helped by the Spirit (Rom 8.14 & 26); and given gifts by the Spirit (1 Cor 12.7). Let us make sure that we do not neglect the gift that is in us.

CHAPTER 5

MODERN PENTECOSTALISM
- Try the spirits whether they are of God

THE MODERN PHENOMENON
The beginnings of modern Pentecostalism are normally traced back to early 20th century Los Angeles. In the year 1906 a holiness preacher, William J. Seymour (1895-1922), became the Pastor of a Holiness Church in Azusa Street, L.A. Later joined by Edward Lee, the two men taught divine healing and glossolalia (speaking in tongues) as a sign of baptism in the Spirit. During the next 10 years, the movement spread worldwide from what became known as the Azusa Street Revival. Another early preacher who figured much was Charles F. Parham, who linked healing to the degree of faith, believing that taking medicines was wrong. Parham, who held a number of unorthodox views, was a white supremacist who objected strongly to the inter-racial meetings that Seymour was promoting. They parted company. Even so, the message of modern-day Spirit-baptism, tongues and healing had instant appeal to many people, and the first wave of Pentecostalism had gone out worldwide.

From those initial beginnings, there were other waves of Pentecostalism in the 1960s, the most famous known as the charismatic renewal. There was a new emphasis on healing, exorcism, and receiving revelations. The excesses of extreme Pentecostalism in Toronto were widely publicised in the 1960s with displays of people falling and rolling, laughing hysterically, making animal sounds amid chaotic scenes of uncontrolled trembling. What was regarded by some as the Toronto blessing, was considered by others as a dangerous manifestation of the flesh - or worse. The advent of YouTube has made it comparatively easy for anyone to research and witness all manner of moderate and extreme Pentecostalism. The Pentecostalists tend to stay within Pentecostal denominational churches, whereas Charismatics can be found throughout other mainstream denominations, including the Roman Catholic Church.

The main common denominator that unites all kinds of Pentecostalists, whether moderate or extreme, is the belief that all the gifts of the Spirit given on the day of Pentecost continue to the present day. For this reason, their theological position regarding gifts is described as **continuationist**. By contrast, the view that some gifts have ceased, such as sign gifts and revelatory gifts, is described as **cessationist**. It is the conviction of this writer, for the reasons already given, that the cessationist view of gifts is the correct and Biblical position.

The continuationist view, combined with a faulty understanding of the baptism of the Spirit, has led the Pentecostal followers to dabble in tongues, continuing revelations, prophecies, healing, signs and wonders, as well as trance-inducing experiences such as being slain in the Spirit. As we observe these practices with the help of the internet, we see very little evidence of Christ-centred worship.

True spiritual worship is not conducted by experiencing an altered state of consciousness. Worship is led by the Spirit with the full faculty of our understanding. Paul states "I will pray with the spirit, and I will pray with the understanding also: I will sing with the spirit and I will sing with the understanding also" (1 Cor 14.15). We hasten to acknowledge that there are many fine believers in the Pentecostal movement, especially among the more moderate groupings. **However,** for the Christian who is seeking local church fellowship according to the New Testament pattern, we strongly and lovingly urge you to make a Bible-based choice rather than an experience-based choice. To that end, we pray that this book might be helpful.

THE MISUNDERSTANDING AND MISUSE OF GIFTS

We can learn lessons, with humility, from the Pentecostalist experience. Instead of understanding the baptism of the Spirit to be uniquely linked to the formation of the church on the day of Pentecost, they misunderstand it to be an extra spiritual blessing to a believer at a time after their conversion. Many pray for this blessing and consider that their prayer has been answered when they apparently start speaking in tongues. Many pray for the 'baptism of the Spirit' but are perplexed when their prayers are not answered. In some circles, meetings descend into chaos with people shaking and dancing in a trance to intoxicating music while crying hysterically in incomprehensible utterings that neither they nor anyone else understands.

The Bible does not invite us to pray for the baptism of the Spirit, but it does urge us to be filled with the Spirit. John Phillips has helpfully observed: "Most of the Holy Spirit's ministries to believers are once-for-all sovereign acts of God. The indwelling, the baptism, the sealing, the earnest, and the gift of the Spirit are in no way dependent on us. They are wrought in us by the Holy Spirit at the time of our conversion; they are irreversible and irrevocable. The filling of the Holy Spirit, however, is different. It is conditional because it depends on our cooperation with the indwelling Spirit of God[9]. According to Paul in Ephesians 5.18-21, the outcome of being filled with the Spirit will be seen, not in chaotic and hysterical behaviour, but in speaking to one another in psalms, hymns, spiritual songs, singing and making melody in

---

[9]Phillips, John Exploring Ephesians (Loizeaux Brothers, NJ 1993) p.153

the heart to the Lord, giving of thanks to God and submitting to one another in the fear of God. Significantly, he mentions nothing about tongues or trance-inducing activities:

"And be not drunk with wine, wherein is excess; but **be filled with the Spirit**; speaking to yourselves in psalms and hymns and spiritual songs, singing and making melody in your heart to the Lord; giving thanks always for all things unto God and the Father in the name of our Lord Jesus Christ; submitting yourselves one to another in the fear of God" (Eph 5.18-21).

In apostolic days there were clear cases of miraculous healing. What happens at modern healing meetings bears no resemblance to what was happening after Pentecost. Peter said to the paralysed man, "In the name of Jesus Christ of Nazareth rise up and walk" (Acts 3.6). The man leaped up, and entered the temple, walking, and leaping, and praising God. This is not what happens at modern healing meetings where people are assisted out of wheelchairs, only to be returned a short time later.

On one occasion in Jerusalem, the twelve apostles were in Solomon's Porch working many signs and wonders among the people. We read that "Insomuch that they brought forth the sick into the streets, and laid them on beds and couches, that at the least the shadow of Peter passing by might overshadow some of them. There came also a multitude out of the cities round about unto Jerusalem, bringing sick folks, and them which were vexed with unclean spirits: and they were healed every one" (Acts 5.15-16). Again, this cannot be compared to the shambolic displays of modern frenzied healing meetings. We certainly believe that God can still heal the sick in answer to prayer, but we reject the notion that there are those today who have the gift of healing as in apostolic times.

While at Lydda near Joppa, the apostle Peter spoke to the dead body of Dorcas "Tabitha, arise" (Acts 9.40). By the power of God, Peter raised a dead woman to life. It is ludicrous to suggest that there are still apostles today who can raise the dead. As for modern pentecostalists claiming that dead people have been raised to life, we judge all such claims as spurious.

Not only have the miraculous gifts passed away, but the revelatory gifts have also ceased. The completed New Testament has replaced the gifts of apostles and prophets whose original work was foundational. When a modern pentecostalist apostle or prophet claims to be delivering an oracle directly from God, we must reject the claim out of hand. Prophets were replaced by teachers when 'that which is perfect' had come.

THE MATTER OF HEADSHIP

There is a further scriptural problem with modern Pentecostalism that we have not yet mentioned in our study. We must address the issue of women taking vocal roles in the church ministry of preaching and teaching. Further, they carry out these activities with their heads uncovered. Quite often a Pentecostal church is co-pastored by a husband-and-wife team. They appeal to 1 Corinthians 11 verse 5 to show that women must have prayed and prophesied in church. That is an unwarranted inference as other references will plainly show that, when we come to an assembled church, the women are clearly forbidden to speak:

> "...as in all churches of the saints. Let your women keep silence in the churches: for it is not permitted unto them to speak; but they are commanded to be under obedience, as also saith the law. And if they will learn any thing, let them ask their husbands at home: for it is a shame for women to speak in the church. What? came the word of God out from you? or came it unto you only? If any man think himself to be a prophet, or spiritual, let him acknowledge that the

things that I write unto you are the commandments of the Lord. But if any man be ignorant, let him be ignorant" (1 Cor 14.33b-38; See also 1 Tim 2.11-12).

These prohibitions cannot be dismissed as cultural. Paul challenges the Corinthian readers to acknowledge that the things he had been writing were the commandments of the Lord. This is a real problem with Pentecostal churches. They have rejected the headship teaching of 1 Corinthians 11 by discarding the head covering for sisters and have disobeyed the other scriptures which plainly forbid women to speak in church.

THE MATTER OF THE GOSPEL

Many Pentecostalists add the healing of the body to the gospel message. Not only does salvation bring the forgiveness of sins but, according to some, it also brings physical healing. However, they add the caveat that healing may not happen in every case. This is confusion. When we preach the gospel faithfully according to John 3.16, God will save sinners. If we add bodily healing and miracles to the message, we will end with spurious professions. When we try to persuade new converts to seek a second blessing by the baptism of the Spirit at a later date, we are further adding to the confusion. These errors stem from the failure to discern that some gifts have ceased with the passing of the first generation of apostles and prophets, whilst 'that which is perfect' has come. The baptism of the Spirit was to do with the birth of the church on the day of Pentecost. When a person trusts in Christ today, he or she is immediately indwelt by the Holy Spirit and added to the church, the body of Christ.

Again, we reiterate that many people in the Pentecostalist movement are soundly saved. We do not wish to offend any true believer, but we certainly want to challenge their assumptions on the gifts of the Holy Spirit and the baptism of the Spirit. This book is submitted to be helpful.

CHAPTER 6

BEYOND THE RAPTURE
- Concluding Summary

THE HOLY SPIRIT IN THE TRIBULATION

The tribulation on earth does not begin until the church has been raptured. Paul tells us that the man of sin will not be revealed until the 'restrainer' is taken out of the way: "For the mystery of lawlessness is already at work; only He who now restrains will do so until He is taken out of the way. And then the lawless one will be revealed..." (2 Thess 2.7-8 NKJV). The restrainer, therefore, we take to be the Spirit-indwelt church. When the church is removed from the earth, there will no longer be in the world a unified body of believers indwelt by the Spirit. We suggest that the Spirit will operate again largely as in Old Testament times, returning to national distinctions and fulfilling national promises to Israel in preparation for the millennium. As the 144,000 go out to preach the gospel of the kingdom, the Spirit will doubtlessly be working with them (Mt 24.14). Those who call on the name of the Lord shall be saved (Joel 2.32) and will be indwelt (individually) by the Spirit (Ez 36.26).

THE HOLY SPIRIT IN THE MILLENNIUM

When the times of the Gentiles are ended, and Christ returns to earth in glory to deliver His people Israel, there will be an outpouring of the Spirit. In those amazing days to come, the words of the prophet Joel will be fulfilled: "And it shall come to pass afterward, that I will pour out my spirit upon all flesh; ... And also upon the servants and upon the handmaids in those days will I pour out my spirit" (Joel 2.28-29). This had an initial fulfilment in Acts 2 regarding the church, but the final fulfilment for the nation will be at the beginning of the millennium on Christ's return. Zechariah also prophesies: "And I will pour upon the house of David, and upon the inhabitants of Jerusalem, the spirit of grace and of supplications" (Zech 12.10). According to Ezekiel, God will also gather His people from the nations, placing them in their own land and putting His Spirit in them: "A new heart also will I give you, and a new spirit will I put within you: and I will take away the stony heart out of your flesh, and I will give you an heart of flesh. And I will put my spirit within you, and cause you to walk in my statutes, and ye shall keep my judgments, and do them" (Ez 36.24-27).

A feature of the Holy Spirit's ministry in Old Testament times was that the Spirit could come upon people and depart from people. By contrast, in this New Testament age, the Spirit is with us, in us, and will never leave us. The church is a 'mystery' people (by which we mean hidden in the Old Testament but now revealed in the New Testament, Ephesians 3.3-6), baptised with the Spirit into the body of Christ. In tribulation times, after the rapture of the church, the Spirit of God will once again operate to bring about the fulfilment of Old Testament prophecies concerning the Messiah, Israel, and the nations. Finally, the leading feature of the millennial age is that there will be a mighty and unprecedented outpouring of the Spirit on all flesh.

CONCLUDING SUMMARY
We began this study by posing the following question: How should we respond to a new convert who says, "I have trusted Christ as

my Saviour and am now waiting and praying for the baptism of the Holy Spirit"? We trust we have respectfully shown that this is a serious misunderstanding of the scriptures. We repeat for clarity: The term 'baptism of the Spirit' refers specifically to the formation of the church on the day of Pentecost, when believers were baptised by the Spirit into the body of Christ. The Lord Jesus said, "I will build my church" (Mt 16.18). From Pentecost to the rapture, every person who trusts Christ immediately receives the indwelling Holy Spirit and is added to the church, His body. It is therefore unnecessary and inappropriate for an individual Christian to pray for the baptism of the Spirit because they have, at their conversion, already come into the good of what took place on the day of Pentecost. The baptism of the Spirit is not some kind of ecstatic experience for which one is to pray, but is an historical event which has already taken place and cannot be repeated. The Christian is not asked to seek the baptism of the Spirit, something he already has, but is urged to be filled with the Spirit, a blessing which should be ongoing in the life of every believer (Eph 5.18).

We trust we have been of some help to any believer who is wanting to understand the important subjects of the baptism of the Spirit and the gifts of the Spirit. We set out some relevant scripture references for the reader's convenience.

a) The Baptism of the Holy Spirit

Viewed prophetically (looking forward to a future event)
- Matthew 3.11
- Mark 1.8
- Luke 3.16
- John 1.33
- Acts 1.5

Viewed doctrinally (looking back to a past event)
- 1 Corinthians 12.13
- Galatians 3.27
- Ephesians 4.5

Viewed historically (looking at events as they happened)
- Acts 2.1-4
- Acts 8.15-17
- Acts 10.44-48 & Acts 11.15-17
- Acts 19.1-6

It is important to understand that the promise of the Father and the baptism of the Holy Spirit took place on the Day of Pentecost when the Holy Spirit came down from heaven and fell on the apostles and every other believer at that time, indwelling them and baptising them into the body of Christ. That was the beginning of the church and, as such, is never repeated.

b) The Gifts of the Holy Spirit

There are four lists of spiritual gifts in the New Testament, and it is important to observe the distinctions in emphasis. The list of spiritual gifts given in 1 Corinthians is not only the longest of the four lists, but is also the earliest in time, and so includes the miraculous and sign gifts. The list in Romans comes later and is reduced to seven in number. The list in Ephesians, which comes latest in order of time, is different in that the gifts are the men given to the church for its edification. J.M. Davies helpfully explains, "In this (Ephesians) passage, written some years later still, there are but five listed, two of which are said to be connected with the laying of the doctrinal foundation, leaving three gifts which are permanent, viz. **the evangelist, the pastor, and the teacher**". The service gifts of Peter are also current today.

c) When That which is Perfect is Come

What does Paul mean by "that which is perfect"? It almost certainly refers to the perfect and inspired writings of the New Testament. In other words, the New Testament scriptures comprise the completed and perfect revelation of Christian doctrine and so supersede the pentecostal gifts of prophecy, tongues and knowledge. The New Testament is basically the apostles' doctrine ratified in written form. The Old and New Testaments together comprise God's wonderful gift to this world, the Bible.

d) References to the Holy Spirit
1) The Baptism, Acts 1.5
2) The Indwelling, 1Corinthians 3.16
3) The Gift, Acts 2.38
4) The Sealing, Ephesians 4.30
5) The Guarantee, Ephesians 1.14
6) The Anointing, 2 Corinthians1.21
7) The Fulness, Ephesians 5.18

e) The Lord's commission to the apostles and to us

"But when the Comforter is come, whom I will send unto you from the Father, even the Spirit of truth, which proceedeth from the Father, **he shall testify of me: and ye also shall bear witness**, because ye have been with me from the beginning" (Jn 15.26-27). May the Holy Spirit guide us into a closer walk with God and an ever-increasing appreciation of our Lord Jesus Christ.

THE FIVE MAJOR REFERENCES TO BAPTISM IN THE BIBLE

	THE BAPTISER	THE CANDIDATE WHO IS BEING BAPTISED	THE ELEMENT IN WHICH (OR WITH WHICH) THE CANDIDATE IS BAPTISED	THE NEW STATUS INTO WHICH (OR UNTO WHICH) THE CANDIDATE IS BAPTISED
1) THE BAPTISM OF MOSES 1 Cor 10.2	This baptism is a historical illustration and is figurative only	All Israel	In the water and in the cloud	Baptised unto Moses
2) JOHN'S BAPTISM Luke 3.16	John the Baptist	A repentant Jew	In, and with, water	Baptised unto repentance
3) THE BAPTISM OF THE HOLY SPIRIT Acts 2.1-4 1 Cor 12.13	The Lord Jesus Christ	The 12 Apostles and all believers in the Lord Jesus on the Day of Pentecost, and subsequently inclusive of all believers.	In, and with, the Holy Spirit	Baptised into the Body of Christ (the Church)
4) BELIEVER'S BAPTISM Rom 6.3	A responsible fellow believer	A new believer	In water	Baptised into the death of Christ and raised to newness of life in Him
5) NOAH'S BAPTISM 1 Peter 3.21	This baptism is a historical illustration and is figurative only	Eight souls, including Noah	Through the Flood	Died to an old world and saved unto a new world

Table 1: The five major references to baptism in the Bible.

CHRONOLOGY OF NEW TESTAMENT LITERATURE

DECADE	WRITING	DATE	PLACE
A.D. 40-50	James	44-49	Jerusalem
50-60	1 Thessalonians	52	Corinth
	2 Thessalonians	53	Corinth
	1 Corinthians (gifts)	57	Ephesus
	2 Corinthians	57	Macedonia
	Galatians	58	Corinth
	Romans (gifts)	58	Corinth
50-70	Mark	50-55	Rome
	Luke	58-61	Caesarea
	Matthew	60-61	Judea
60-70	Ephesians (gifts)	62-63	Rome
	Colossians	62-63	Rome
	Philemon	62-63	Rome
	Philippians	63	Rome
	1 Peter (gifts)	62-64	Babylon?
	Acts	63-64	Rome
	Hebrews	64-68	Rome?
	2 Peter	64-68	Rome?
	Jude	65-68	Jerusalem
	1 Timothy	65-67	Macedonia
	Titus	65-67	Ephesus?
	2 Timothy	67-68	Rome
	Revelation	68-70	Patmos
90-100	John's Gospel	90-95	Ephesus
	John's Epistles	90-98	Ephesus

Table 2: Chronology of New Testament literature
(Source: *Know your Bible* by W. Graham Scroggie)

THE FEASTS OF JEHOVAH

FEAST	HISTORICAL MEANING FOR ISRAEL	DOCTRINAL AND PROPHETIC MEANING
Feast of Passover	Redemption out of Egypt	Death of Christ and redemption through His blood
Feast of Unleavened Bread	The night of deliverance (*Obligatory feast for all males*)	Fellowship of saints
Feast of First Fruits (of barley harvest)	To honour God and thank Him for the harvest to come. God's pledge of the harvest.	Resurrection of Christ from the dead. Christ the first fruits (1 Cor 15.23)
Feast of Pentecost or Feast of Weeks or Harvest (of wheat)	To thank God for the wheat harvest (*Obligatory feast for all males*)	The coming of the Holy Spirit and the formation of the church
None	None	Interval speaking of this present age
Feast of Trumpets	To prepare and rally for the final feasts	The Gospel of the Kingdom
The Day of Atonement	Annual cleansing	1) The death of Christ 2) The national cleansing of Israel
Feast of Tabernacles	The final ingathering. To recall the wilderness experience. (*Obligatory feast for all males*)	The millennium

Table 3: The Feasts of Jehovah.
The Lord Jesus died on the Feast of Passover and rose from the dead on the Feast of First Fruits. After 50 days, the Holy Spirit came down on the Feast of Pentecost.

BIBLIOGRAPHY

DAVIES, J.M., *Collected writings of J.M.Davies, Volume 1, Pentecost and today, pp.239-305; also The Christian's Statue of Liberty p.464.* (Cookstown, N.Ireland: Scripture Teaching Library, 2014)

HOSTE, WILLIAM & RODGERS, WILLIAM, *Bible problems and answers,* see answer to question *What do the words "When that which is perfect is come," (1 Cor 13.10) mean? p.331* W.H. (Kilmarnock, John Ritchie Ltd, 1986)

HUNTER, J., *1 Corinthians* in *What The Bible Teaches,* see comment on 1 Cor. 13.10 (Kilmarnock, John Ritchie Ltd, 1986)

MacDONALD, William, *Believer's Bible Commentary,* see comment on 1 Cor. 13:10 (Nashville, Thomas Nelson Publishers, 1995)

SAXE, RAYMOND H., *Partial or Perfect? The cessation of signs and completeness of scripture* (Lisburn, N.Ireland: Scripture Teaching Library, 2013)

SCROGGIE, W.GRAHAM, *The Baptism of the Spirit and Speaking with Tongues* (London, Pickering & Inglis Ltd., 1956)

SILVA, J.W. de, *The Charismatic Challenge: A Biblical Investigation* (Kilmarnock, John Ritchie Ltd, 1999)

VINE, W.E., *1 Corinthians* in *The Collected Writings of W.E.Vine Volume 2,* see comment on 1 Cor 13.10 (Glasgow, Gospel Tract Publications, 1985)

VINE, W.E., *1 & 2 Timothy* in *The Collected Writings of W.E.Vine Volume 3,* see comments on 1 Tim 4.14 and 2 Tim 1.6 (Glasgow, Gospel Tract Publications, 1985)

VINE, W.E, *Expository Dictionary of Bible Words* (London, Marshall Morgan & Scott, 1980)